WHY I DO NOT
IN GOD.

BY

ANNIE BESANT.

LONDON:

FREETHOUGHT PUBLISHING COMPANY,

63, FLEET STREET, E.C.

1887.

———

PRICE THREEPENCE.

LONDON :

PRINTED BY ANNIE BESANT AND CHARLES BRADLAUGH,
63, FLEET STREET, E.C.

WHY I DO NOT BELIEVE IN GOD.

THERE is no doubt that the majority of people in most parts of the world—save in those in which Buddhism is supreme—believe in the existence of a God. The kind of God may vary indefinitely, but there is generally "some God or other". Now a growing minority in every civilised country finds it intellectually impossible to make the affirmation which is necessary for belief in God, and this growing minority includes many of the most thoughtful and most competent minds. The refusal to believe is unfortunately not always public, so cruel is the vengeance worked by society on those who do not bow down to its fetishes; but as John Stuart Mill said: "The world would be astonished if it knew how great a proportion of its brightest ornaments—of those most distinguished even in popular estimation for wisdom and virtue—are complete sceptics in religion" ("Autobiography," p. 45).

It is sad that all should not recognise that, as the late Professor Clifford put it, Truth is a thing to be shouted from the housetops, not to be whispered over the walnuts and wine after the ladies have left; for only by plain and honest speech on this matter can liberty of thought be won. Each who speaks out makes easier speech for others, and none, however insignificant, has right of silence here. Nor is it unfair, I think, that a minority should be challenged on its dissidency, and should be expected to state clearly and definitely the grounds of its disagreement with the majority.

Ere going into detailed argument it may be well to remind the reader that the burden of affording proof lies on the affirmer of a proposition; the rational attitude of the human mind is not that of a boundless credulity, accepting every statement as true until it has been proved to be false, but is that of a suspension of judgment on every statement which, though not obviously false, is not supported by evidence, and of an absolute rejection of a statement self-contradictory in its terms, or incompatible with truths already demonstrated. To remove this position from the region of prejudice in which theological discussion is carried on, it may be well to take the following illustration: a man asks me, "Do you believe that Jupiter is inhabited by a race of men who have one eye in the middle of their foreheads, and who walk about on three legs, with their heads under their left arms?" I answer: "No, I do not believe it; I have no evidence that such beings exist". If my interlocutor desires to convince me that Jupiter has inhabitants, and that his description of them is accurate, it is for him to bring forward evidence in support of his contention. The burden of proof evidently lies on him; it is not for me to prove that no such beings exist before my non-belief is justified, but for him to prove that they do exist before my belief can be fairly claimed. Similarly, it is for the affirmer of God's existence to bring evidence in support of his affirmation; the burden of proof lies on him.

For be it remembered that the Atheist makes no general denial of the existence of God; he does not say, "There is no God". If he put forward such a proposition, which he can only do intelligently if he understand the term "God", then, truly, he would be bound to bring forth his evidence in support. But the proof of a universal negative requires the possession of perfect knowledge of the universe of discourse, and in this case the universe of discourse is conterminous with the totality of existence. No man can rationally affirm "There is no God", until the word "God" has for him a definite meaning, and until everything that exists is known to him, and known with what Leibnitz calls "perfect knowledge". The Atheist's denial of the Gods begins only when these Gods are defined or described. Never yet has a God been defined in terms which were not palpably self-contradictory and absurd; never yet has a God been described so that a concept of him was made possible to human thought. Again I fall back on an illustration unconnected with theology in order to make clearly apparent the distinction drawn. If I am asked: "Do you believe in the existence of a triangle in space on the other side of Saturn?" I answer, "I neither believe in, nor deny its existence; I know nothing about it". But if I am asked: "Do you believe in the existence there of a boundless triangle, or of a square triangle?" then my answer is: "I deny the possibility of the existence of such triangles". The reason for the different answers to the two questions is that as I have never visited the other side of Saturn I know nothing about the existence or non-existence of triangles there; but I deny the possibility of the existence of a boundless triangle, because the word triangle means a figure enclosed by three limiting lines; and I deny the possibility of the existence of a square triangle, because a triangle has three sides only while a square has four, and all the angles of a triangle taken together are equal to two right angles, while those of a square are equal to four. I allege that anyone who believes in a square triangle can have no clear concept either of a triangle or of a square. And so while I refuse to say "there is no God", lacking the knowledge which would justify the denial, since to me the word God represents no concept, I do say, "there is no infinite personality, there is no infinite creator, there is no being at once almighty and all-good, there is no Trinity in Unity, there is no eternal and infinite existence save that of which each one of us is mode". For be it noted, these denials are justified by our knowledge: an undefined "God" might be a limited being on the far side of Sirius, and I have no knowledge which justifies me in denying such an existence; but an infinite God, *i.e.*, a God who is everywhere, who has no limits, and yet who is not I and who is therefore limited by my personality, is a being who is self-contradictory, both limited and not-limited, and such a being cannot exist. No perfect knowledge is needed here. "God is an infinite being" is disproved by one being who is not God. "God is everywhere" is disproved by the finding of one spot where God is not. The universal affirmative is disproved by a single exception. Nor is anything gained by the assertors of deity when they allege that he is incomprehensible. If "God" exists and is incomprehensible, his incomprehensibility is an admirable reason for being silent about him, but can never justify the affirmation of self-contradictory propositions, and the threatening of people with damnation if they do not accept them.

I turn to examine the evidence which is brought forward

in support of the existence of God, taking "God" to mean
some undefined being other than and superior to the
various forms of living and non-living things on this
earth—or those forming part of the "material universe"
in which we exist—and related to these as creator and
controller.   Now the existence of anything may be sensated or it may be inferred; the astronomer believed in
the existence of Saturn because he saw it; but he also
believed in the existence of the planet afterwards named
Neptune before he saw it, attaining this belief by way of
induction from the otherwise inexplicable behavior of
Uranus.   Can we then by the senses or by the reason find
out God?

The most common, and to many the most satisfactory
and convincing evidence, is that of the senses.   A child
born into the world has open to him these sense avenues
of knowledge; he learns that something exists which is
not he by the impressions made on his senses; he sees, he
feels, he hears, he smells, he tastes, and thus he learns to
know.   As the child's past and present sensations increase
in number, as he begins to remember them, to compare,
to mark likenesses and unlikenesses, he gathers the
materials for further mental elaboration.   But this sen-
sational basis of his knowledge is the limit of the area on
which his intellectual edifice can be built; he may rear it
upward as far as his powers will permit, but he can never
widen his foundation, while his senses remain only what
they are.   All that the mind works on has reached it by
these senses; it can dissociate and combine, it can break
in pieces and build up, but no sensation no percept, and
no percept no concept.

When this fundamental truth is securely grasped it will
be seen of what tremendous import is the admitted fact
that the senses wholly fail us when we seek for proof of
the existence of God.   Our belief in the existence of all
things outside ourselves rests on the testimony of the
senses.   The "objective universe" is that which we sensate.   When we reason and reflect, when we think of love,
and fear, when we speak of truth and honor, we know
that all these are not susceptible of being sensated, that
is, that they have no objective existence; they belong to
the Subject universe.   Now if God cannot be sensated he
also must belong to the Subject world; that is, he must

be a creation of the mind, with no outside corresponding reality.   Granted that we can never know "the thing in itself"; granted that all we know is only the effect on the mind produced by something which differs from the effect it produces; yet this fundamental physiological distinction remains between the Object and the Subject worlds, that the Object world announces itself by nervous action which is set up at the periphery, while the Subject world results from the centrally initiated travail of the brain.

It might, indeed, be argued by the Theist that God may exist, but may be incognisable by our senses, we lacking the sense which might sensate deity.   Quite so.   There may be existences around us but unknown to us, there being no part of our organism differentiated to receive from them impressions.   There are rays beyond the solar spectrum which are invisible to us normally, the existence of which was unknown to us some years ago, but some of which apparently serve among light rays for the ant; so there may be all kinds of existences in the universe of which we are unconscious, as unconscious as we were of the existence of the ultra-violet rays until a chemical reagent rendered them visible.   But as we cannot sensate them, *for us they do not exist*.   This, then, cannot avail the Theist, for an incognisable God, a God who can enter into no kind of relation with us, is to us a non-existent God.   We cannot even conceive a sense entirely different from those we possess, let alone argue over what we should find out by means of it if we had it.

It is said that of old time the evidence of the senses for the existence of God was available; the seventy elders "saw the God of Israel"; Moses talked with him "face to face"; Elijah heard his "still small voice".   But these experiences are all traditional; we have no evidence at first hand; no witness that we can examine; no facts that we can investigate.   There is not even evidence enough to start a respectable ghost story, let alone enough to bear the tremendous weight of the existence of God.   Yet, if some finite "God" exist—I say finite, because, as noted above, the co-existence of an infinite God and a finite creature is impossible—how easy for him to prove his existence; if he be too great for our "comprehension", as some Theists argue, he might surely bestow on us a sense which might receive impressions from him, and enable us to reach at least a partial, an imperfect, knowledge of him. But if he exist, he wraps himself in darkness; if he exist, he folds himself in silence. Leaning, as it were, over the edge of being, men strive to pierce the dark abyss of the unknown, above, below; they strain their sight, but they see nothing; they listen, but nothing strikes their ear; weary, dizzy, they stagger backwards, and with the darkness pressing on their eyeballs they murmur "God!".

Failing to discover God by way of the senses, we turn to such evidence for his existence as may be found by way of the reason, in order to determine whether we can establish by inference that which we have failed to establish by direct proof.

As the world is alleged to be the handiwork of God, it is not unreasonable to scrutinise the phænomena of nature, and to seek in them for traces of a ruling intelligence, of a guiding will. But it is impossible even to glance at natural phænomena, much less to study them attentively, without being struck by the enormous waste of energy, the aimless destruction, the utterly unintelligent play of conflicting and jarring forces. For centuries "nature" has been steadily at work growing forests, cutting out channels for rivers, spreading alluvial soil and clothing it with grass and flowers; at last a magnificent landscape is formed, birds and beasts dwell in its woods and on its pastures, men till its fertile fields, and thank the gracious God they worship for the work of his hands; there is a far-off growl which swells as it approaches, a trembling of the solid earth, a crash, an explosion, and then, in a darkness lightened only by the fiery rain of burning lava, all beauty, all fertility, vanish, and the slow results of thousands of years are destroyed in a night of earthquake and volcanic fury. Is it from this wild destruction of slowly obtained utility that we are to infer the existence of a divine intelligence and divine will? If beauty and use were aimed at, why the destruction? If desolation and uselessness, why the millenniums spent in growth?

During the year 1886 many hundreds of people in Greece, in Spain, in America, in New Zealand, were killed or maimed by earthquakes and by cyclones. Many more perished in hurricanes at sea. Many more by explosions in mines and elsewhere. These deaths caused widespread misery, consigned families to hopeless poverty, cut short careers of use and of promise. They were caused by "natural" forces. Is "God" behind nature, and are all these horrors planned, carried out, by his mind and will? John Stuart Mill has put the case clearly and forcibly :

"Next to the greatness of these cosmic forces, the quality which most forcibly strikes everyone who does not avert his eyes from it is their perfect and absolute recklessness. They go straight to their end, without regarding what or whom they crush on the road. Optimists, in their attempts to prove that 'whatever is, is right', are obliged to maintain, not that nature ever turns one step from her path to avoid trampling us into destruction, but that it would be very unreasonable in us to expect that she should. Pope's 'Shall gravitation cease when you go by?' may be a just rebuke to anyone who should be so silly as to expect common human morality from nature. But if the question were between two men, instead of between a man and a natural phænomenon, that triumphant apostrophe would be thought a rare piece of impudence. A man who should persist in hurling stones or firing cannon when another man 'goes by', and having killed him should urge a similar plea in exculpation, would very deservedly be found guilty of murder. In sober truth, nearly all the things which men are hanged or imprisoned for doing to one another, are Nature's everyday performances. Killing, the most criminal act recognised by human laws, Nature does once to every being that lives; and in a large proportion of cases, after protracted tortures such as only the greatest monsters whom we read of ever purposely inflicted on their living fellow creatures. If, by an arbitrary reservation, we refuse to account anything murder but what abridges a certain term supposed to be allotted to human life, nature also does this to all but a small percentage of lives, and does it in all the modes, violent or insidious, in which the worst human beings take the lives of one another. Nature impales men, breaks them as if on the wheel, casts them to be devoured by wild beasts, burns them to death, crushes them with stones like the first Christian martyr, starves them with hunger, freezes them with cold, poisons them by the quick or slow venom of her exhalations, and has hundreds of other hideous deaths in reserve, such as the ingenious cruelty of a Nabis or a Domitian never surpassed. All this, Nature does with the most supercilious disregard both of mercy and of justice, emptying her shafts upon the best and noblest indifferently with the meanest and worst; upon those who are engaged in the highest and worthiest enterprises, and often as the direct consequence of the noblest acts; and it might almost be imagined as a punishment for them. She mows down those on whose existence hangs the wellbeing of a whole people, perhaps the prospects of the human race for generations to come, with as little compunction as those whose death is a relief to themselves, or a blessing to those under their noxious influence" ("Three Essays on Religion," pp. 28, 29, ed. 1874).

It is not only from the suffering caused by the undeviating course of the phænomena which from the invariable sequence of their happening are called "laws of nature" that we infer the absence of any director or controller of these forces. There are many absurdities as well as miseries, caused by the "uniformity of nature". Dr. Büchner tells us of a kid he saw which was born perfect in all parts save that it was headless ("Force and Matter", page 234, ed. 1884). Here, for weeks the kid was a-forming, although life in the outer world was impossible for it. Monstrosities occur in considerable numbers, and each one bears silent witness to the unintelligence of the forces that produced it. Nay, they can be artificially produced, as has been shown by a whole series of experiments, eggs tapped during incubation yielding monstrous chickens. In all these cases we recognise the blind action of unconscious forces bringing about a ridiculous and unforeseen result, if turned slightly out of their normal course. From studying this aspect of nature it is certain that we cannot find God. So far from finding here a God to worship, the whole progress of man depends on his learning to control and regulate these natural forces, so as to prevent them from working mischief and to turn them into channels in which they will work for good.

If from scrutinising the forces of nature we study the history of the evolution of life on our globe, and the physical conditions under which man now exists, it is impossible from these to infer the existence of a benevolent power as the creator of the world. Life is one vast battlefield, in which the victory is always to the strong. More organisms are produced than can grow to maturity; they fight for the limited supply of food, and by means of this struggle the weakest are crushed out and the fittest survive to propagate their race. Each successful organism stands on the corpses of its weaker antagonists, and only by this ceaseless strife and slaying has progress been possible. As the organisms grow more complex and more developed, added difficulties surround their existence; the young of the higher animals are weaker and more defenceless at birth than those of the lower, and the young of man, the highest animal yet evolved, is the most helpless of all, and his hold of life the most precarious during infancy. So clumsy is the "plan of creation" that among the most highly-evolved animals a new life is only possible by peril to life already existing, and the mother must pass through long weeks of physical weariness and hours of acute agony ere she can hold her baby in her arms. All these things are so "natural" to us that we need to think of them, not as necessary, but as deliberately planned by a creative power, ere we can realise the monstrous absurdity of supposing them to be the outcome of "design". Nor must we overlook the sufferings caused by the incomplete adaptation of evolving animals to the conditions among which they are developing. The human race is still suffering from its want of adaptation to the upright position, from its inheritance of a structure from quadrupedal ancestors which was suited to the horizontal position of their trunks, but is unsuited to the vertical position of man. The sufferings caused by child-birth, and by hernia, testify to the incomplete adaptation of the race to the upright condition. To believe that all the slow stages of blood-stained evolution, that the struggle for existence, that the survival of the fittest with its other side, the crushing of the less fit, together with a million subsidiary consequences of the main "plan", to believe that all these were designed, foreseen, deliberately selected as the method of creation, by an almighty power, to believe this is to believe that "God" is the supreme malignity, a creator who voluntarily devises and executes a plan of the most ghastly malice, and who works it out with a cruelty in details which no human pen can adequately describe.

But, again, the condition and the history of the world are not consistent with its being the creation of an almighty and perfect cruelty. While the tragedy of life negates the possibility of an omnipotent goodness as its author, the beauty and happiness of life negate equally the possibility of an almighty fiend as its creator. The delight of bird and beast in the vigor of their eager life; the love-notes of mate to mate, and the brooding ectasy of the mother over her young; the rapture of the song which sets quivering the body of the lark as he soars upwards in the sun-rays; the gambols of the young, with every curve telling of sheer joy in life and movement; the beauty and strength of man and woman; the power of intellect, the glory of genius, the exquisite happiness of sympathy; all these things could not find place in the handiwork of a power delighting in pain. We cannot, then, from the study of life on our globe infer the existence of a God who is wholly good; the evil disproves him: nor can we infer the existence of a God who is wholly evil; the good disproves him. All that we learn from life-conditions is that if the world has a creator his character must be exceedingly mixed, and must be one to be regarded with extreme suspicion and apprehension. Be it noted, however, that, so far, we have found no reason to infer the existence of any creative intelligence.

Leaving the phænomena of nature exclusive of man, as yielding us no information as to the existence of God, we turn next to human life and human history to seek for traces of the "divine presence". But here again we are met by the same mingling of good and evil, the same waste, the same prodigality, which met us in non-human nature. Instead of the "Providence watching over the affairs of men" in which Theists believe, we note that "there be just men, unto whom it happeneth according to the work of the wicked; again, there be wicked men, to whom it happeneth according to the work of the righteous". A railway accident happens, in which a useful man, the mainstay of a family, is killed, and from which a profligate escapes. An explosion in a mine slays the hardworking breadwinners at their toil, and the drunken idler whose night's debauch has resulted in heavy morning sleep is "providentially" saved as he snores lazily at home in bed. The man whose life is invaluable to a nation perishes in his prime, while the selfish race-haunting aristocrat lives on to a green old age. The honest conscientious trader keeps with difficulty out of the bankruptcy court, and sees his smart, unscrupulous neighbor pile up a fortune by tricks that just escape the meshes of the law. If indeed there be a guiding hand amid the vicissitudes of human life, it must be that of an ironical, mocking cruelty, which plays with men as puppets for the gratification of a sardonic humor. Of course, the real explanation of all these things is that there is no common factor in these moral and physical propositions; the quantities are incommensurable; the virtues or vices of a man are not among the causes which launch, or do not launch, a chimney pot at his head.

Outside these "changes and chances" of human life, the thoughtful mind feels conscious of a profound dissatisfaction with many of the inevitable conditions of human existence: the sensative faculties are at their keenest when the intelligence is not sufficiently developed to utilise them; the perceptive faculties begin to fail as the reflective touch their fullest development; and when experience is ripest, judgment most trained, knowledge most full, old age lays its palsy on the brain, and senility shakes down the edifice just when a life's toil has made it of priceless value. To recognise our limitations, to accept the inevitable, to amend —so far as amendment is possible—both ourselves and our environment, all this forms part of a rational philosophy of life; but what has such self-controlled and keen-eyed sternness of resolve to do with hysterical outcries for help to some power outside nature, which, if it existed as creator, must have modelled our existence at its pleasure, and towards which our attitude could be only one of bitterest, if silent, rebellion? To bow to the inevitable evil, while studying its conditions in order to strive to make it the evitable, is consistent with strong hope which lightens life's darkness; but to yield crushed before evil deliberately and consciously inflicted by an omnipotent intelligence—in such fate lies the agony of madness and despair.

Nor do we find any reliable signs of the presence of a God in glancing over the incidents of human history. We note unjust wars, in which right is crushed by might, in which victory sides with "the strongest battalions", in the issue of which there appears no trace of a "God that judgeth the earth". We meet with cruelties that sicken us inflicted on man by man; butcheries that desolate a city, persecutions that lay waste a province. In every civilised land of to-day we see wealth mocking poverty, and poverty cursing wealth; here, thousands wasted on a harlot, and there children sobbing themselves in hunger to sleep. Our earth rolls wailing yearly round the sun, bearing evidence that it has no creator who loves and guides it, but has only its men, children of its own womb, who by the ceaseless toil of countless generations are hewing out the possibility of a better and gladder world.

Similar testimony is borne by the slow progress of the human race. Truth is always fighting; each new truth undergoes a veritable struggle for existence, and if Hercules is to live to perform his labors he must succeed in strangling the serpents that hiss round his cradle. The new truth must first be held only by one, its discoverer; if he is not crushed at the outset, a few disciples are won; then the little band is persecuted, some are martyred, and, it may be, the movement destroyed. Or, some survive, and gain converts, and so the new truth slowly spreads, winning acceptance at the last. But each new truth must pass through similar ordeal, and hence the slowness of the upward climb of man. Look backwards over the time which has passed since man was emerging from the brute, and then compare those millenniums with the progress that has been made, and the distance which still separates the race from a reasonably happy life for all its members. If a God cannot do better for man than this, man may be well content to trust to his own unaided efforts. We turn from the phænomena of human life, as from those of non-human nature, without finding any evidence which demonstrates, or even renders probable, the existence of a God.

There is another line of reasoning, however, apart from the consideration of phænomena, which must, it is alleged, lead us to believe in the existence of a God. This is the well-used argument from causation. Every effect must have a cause, therefore the universe must have a cause, is a favorite enthymeme, of which the suppressed minor is, the universe is an effect. But this is a mere begging of the question. Every effect must have a cause; granted; for a cause is defined as that which produces an effect, and an effect as that which is produced by a cause; the two words are co-relatives, and the one is meaningless separated from the other. Prove that the universe is an effect, and in so doing you will have proved that it has a cause; but in the proof of that quietly-suppressed minor is the *crux* of the dispute. We see that the forces around us are the causes of various effects, and that they, the causes of events which follow their action, are themselves the effects of causes which preceded such action. From the continued observation of these sequences, ourselves part of this endless chain, the idea of causation is worked into the human mind, and becomes, as it were, part of its very texture, so that we cannot in thought separate phænomena from their causes, and the uncaused becomes to us the inconceivable. But we cannot rationally extend reasoning wholly based on phænomena into the region of the noumenon. That which is true of the phænomenal universe gives us no clue when we try to pass without it, and to penetrate into the mystery of existence *per se*. To call God "the first cause" is to play with words after their meaning has been emptied from them. If the argument from causation is to be applied to the existence of the universe, which is, without any proof, to be accepted as an effect, why may it not with equal force be applied to "God", who, equally without any proof, may be regarded as an effect? and so we may create an illimitable series of Gods, each an assumption unsupported by evidence. If we once begin puffing divine smoke-rings, the only limit to the exercise is our want of occupation and the amount of suitable tobacco our imagination is able to supply. The belief of the Atheist stops where his evidence stops. He believes in the existence of the universe, judging the accessible proof thereof to be adequate, and he finds in this universe sufficient cause for the happening of all phænomena. He finds no intellectual satisfaction in placing a gigantic conundrum behind the universe, which only adds its own unintelligibility to the already sufficiently difficult problem of existence. Our lungs are not fitted to breathe beyond the atmosphere which surrounds our globe, and our faculties cannot breathe outside the atmosphere of the phænomenal. If I went up in a balloon I should check it when I found it carrying me into air too rare for my respiration; and I decline to be carried by a theological balloon into regions wherein thought cannot breathe healthily, but can only fall down gasping, imagining that its gasps are inspiration.

There remain for us to investigate two lines of evidence, either of which suffices, apparently, to carry conviction to a large number of minds; these are, the argument from human experience, and the argument from design.

I have no desire to lessen the weight of an argument drawn from the *sensus communis*, the common sense, of mankind. It is on this that we largely rely in drawing

distinctions between the normal and the abnormal; it is
this which serves as test between the sane and the insane;
no thoughtful student can venture to ignore the tremendous force of the consensus of human experience.
But while he will not ignore, he must judge: he must
ask, first, is this experience universal and unanimous?
Secondly, on what experimental or other evidence is it
based? The universal and unanimous verdict of human
experience, based on clear verifiable experience, is one
which the thinker will challenge with extreme hesitation.
Yet cause may arise which justifies such challenge.
Perhaps no belief has at once been so general, and so
undeniably based on the evidence of the senses, as the
belief in the movement of the sun and the immobility of
our globe. All but the blind could daily see the rising of
the sun in the eastern sky, and its setting in the west; all
could feel the firmness of the unshaken earth, the solid
unmoving steadfastness of the ground on which we tread.
Yet this consensus of human experience, this universality
of human testimony, has been rejected as false on evidence
which none who can feel the force of reasoning is able to
deny. If this belief, in defence of which can be brought
the *ne plus ultra* of the verdict of common sense, be not
tenable in the light of modern knowledge, how shall a
belief on which the *sensus communis* is practically non-
existent, on which human testimony is lacking in many
cases, contradictory in all others, and which fails to maintain itself on experimental or other evidence, how shall it
hold ground from which the other has been driven?

The reply to the question, "Is the evidence universal
and unanimous?" must be in the negative. The religion
of Buddha, which is embraced by more than a third of the
population of the globe, is an Atheistic creed; many
Buddhists pay veneration to Buddha, and to the statues of
their own deceased ancestors, but none pretend that these
objects of reverence are symbols of a divine power. Many
of the lower savage tribes have no idea of God. Darwin
writes: "There is ample evidence, derived not from hasty
travellers, but from men who have long resided with
savages, that numerous races have existed, and still exist,
who have no idea of one or more Gods, and who have no
words in their language to express such an idea" ("Descent
of Man," pp. 93, 94, ed. 1875). Büchner ("Force and

Matter," pp. 382—393) has collected a mass of evidence showing that whole races of men have no idea of God at all. Sir John Lubbock has done the same. When savages reach a stage of intelligence at which they begin to seek the causes of phænomena, they invariably postulate many Gods as causes of the many objects around them. A New Zealander who was told of the existence of the one God by a missionary, asked him scoffingly if, among Europeans, one man made things of every sort; and he argued that as there were various trades among men, so there were various Gods, each with his own business, and one made trees, another the sea, another the animals, and so on. Only when intelligence has reached a comparatively high plane, is evolved the idea of one God, the creator and the ruler of the universe. Moreover this idea of "God" is essentially an abstract, not a concrete idea, and the fancy that there is an entity belonging to it is but a survival of Realism, a theory which is discredited in everything save in this one theological remnant.

It has been alleged by some writers that, however degraded may be the savage, he still has some idea of supernatural existences, and that error on this head has arisen from the want of thoroughly understanding the savage's ideas. But even these writers do not allege that the belief of these savages touches on a being who can be called by the most extreme courtesy "God". There may be a vague fear of the unknown, a tendency to crouch before striking and dangerous manifestations of natural forces, an idea of some unseen power residing in a stone or a relic—a fetish; but such things—and of the existence of even these in the lowest savages evidence is lacking—can surely not be described as belief in God.

Not only is the universal evidence a-wanting, but such evidence as there is wholly lacks unanimity. What attribute of the divine character, what property of the divine nature, is attested by the unanimous voice of human experience? What is there in common between the Mumbo-Jumbo of Africa, and the "heavenly Father", of refined nineteenth century European Theism? What tie, save that of a common name, unites the blood-dripping Tezcatlepoca of Mexico with him "whose tender mercy is over all his works"? Even if we confine ourselves to the Gods of the Jews, the Christians, and the Mahommedans,

how great is the clash of dissension. The Jew proclaims
it blasphemy to speak of a divine Trinity, and shrinks
with horror from the thought of an incarnate God. The
Christian calls it blasphemy to deny the deity of the man
Christ Jesus, and affirms, under anathema, the triune
nature of the Godhead. The Mahommedan asserts the
unity of God, and stamps as infidel everyone who refuses
to see in Mahommed the true revealer of the divinity.
Each is equally certain that he is right, and each is
equally certain that the others are wrong, and are in peril
of eternal damnation for their rejection of the one true
faith. If the Christian has his lake of fire and brimstone
for those who deny Christ, the Mahommedan has his drinks
of boiling water for those who assert him. Among this
clash of tongues, to whom shall turn the bewildered
enquirer after truth? All his would-be teachers are
equally positive, and equally without evidence. All are
loud in assertion, but singularly modest in their offers of
proof.

Now, it may be taken as an undeniable fact that where
there is confusion of belief there is deficiency of evidence.
Scientific men quarrel and dispute over some much con-
troverted scientific theory. They dispute because the
experimental proofs are lacking that would decide the
truth or the error of the suggested hypothesis. While
the evidence is unsatisfactory, the controversy continues,
but when once decisive proof has been discovered all
tongues are still. The endless controversies over the existence of God show that decisive proof has not yet been
attained. And while this proof is wanting, I remain
Atheist, resolute not to profess belief till my intellect can
find some stable ground whereon to rest.

We have reached the last citadel, once the apparently
impregnable fortress of Theism, but one whose walls are
now crumbling, the argument from design. It was this
argument which so impressed John Stuart Mill that he
wrote in his Essay on "Theism": "I think it must be
allowed that, in the present state of our knowledge, the
adaptations in Nature afford a large balance of probability
in favor of creation by intelligence. It is equally certain
that this is no more than a probability" ("Three Essays
on Religion", p. 174). This Essay was, however, written
between the years 1868 and 1870, and at that time the

tremendous effect of the hypothesis of evolution had not yet made itself felt; Mill speaks (p. 172) of the "recent speculations" on "the principle of the 'survival of the of the fittest'", and recognising that if this principle were sound "there would be a constant though slow general improvement of the type as it branched out into many different varieties, adapting it to different media and modes of existence, until it might possibly, in countless ages, attain to the most advanced examples which now exist" (p. 173), he admits that if this be true "it must be acknowledged that it would greatly attenuate the evidence for" creation. And I am prepared to admit frankly that until the "how" of evolution explained the adaptations in Nature, the weight of the argument from design was very great, and to most minds would have been absolutely decisive. It would not of course prove the existence of an omnipotent and universal creator, but it certainly did powerfully suggest the presence of some contriving intelligence at work on natural phænomena. But now, when we can trace the gradual evolution of a complex and highly developed organ through the various stages which separate its origin from its most complete condition; when we can study the retrogression of organs becoming rudimentary by disuse, and the improvement of organs becoming developed by use; when we notice as imperfections in the higher type things which were essential in the lower: what wonder is it that the instructed can no longer admit the force of the argument from design?

The human eye has often been pointed to as a triumphant proof of design, and it naturally seemed perfect in the past to those who could imagine no higher kind of optical instrument; but now, as Tyndall says, "A long list of indictments might indeed be brought against the eye—its opacity, its want of symmetry, its lack of achromatism, its absolute blindness, in part. All these taken together caused Helmholtz to say that, if any optician sent him an instrument so full of defects, he would be justified in sending it back with the severest censure" ("On Light", p. 8, ed. 1875). It is only since men have made optical instruments without the faults of the eye, that we have become aware how much better we might see than we do. Nor is this all; the imperfections which would show incompetence on the part of a designer become interesting and significant as traces of gradual development, and the eye, which in the complexity of its highest form seemed, notwithstanding its defects, to demand such great intelligence to conceive and fashion it, becomes more intelligible when we can watch it a-building, and, as it were, see it put together bit by bit. I venture to quote here from a pamphlet of my own a very brief statement of the stages through which the eye has passed in its evolution: "The first definite eye-spot that we yet know of is a little colored speck at the base of the tentacles of some of the Hydromedusæ, jelly-fish in common parlance. They are only spots of pigment, and we should not know they were attempts at eyes were it not that some relations, the Discophora, have little refractive bodies in their pigment spots, and these refractive bodies resemble the crystalline cones of animals a little higher in the scale. In the next class (Vermes), including all worms, we find only pigment spots in the lowest; then pigment spots with a nerve-fibre ending in them; pigment spots with rod-shaped cells, with crystalline rods; pigment spots with crystalline cones. Next, the cones begin to be arranged radially; and in the Alciopidæ the eye has become a sphere with a lens and a vitreous body, layer of pigment, layer of rods, and optic nerve. To mark the evolution definitely in another way, we find the more highly developed eye of the adult appearing as a pigment spot in the embryo, so that both the evolution of the race and the evolution of the individual tell the same story. In the Echinoderma (sea-urchins, star-fishes) we find only pigment spots in the lower forms, but in the higher the rod-shaped cells, the transparent cones projecting from pigment cells. In the Arthropoda (lobsters, insects, etc.,) the advance continues from the Vermes. The retina is formed more definitely than in the Alciopidæ, and the eye becomes more complex. The compound eye is an attempt at grouping many cones together, and is found in the higher members of this sub-kingdom. In the lowest vertebrate, the Amphioxus, the eye is a mere pigment spot, but in the others the more complex forms are taken up and carried on to the comparative perfection of the mammalian eye" ("Eyes and Ears", pp. 9, 10). And be it noted that in the most complex and highly developed eye there is still the same relation of pigment layer, rod layer, cone layer, seen in its earliest beginnings in the Discophora and the worms.

The line of argument here applied to the eye may be followed in every instance of so-called design. The exquisite mechanism of the ear may be similarly traced, from the mere sac with otoliths of the Medusæ up to the elaborate external, middle, and internal ears of man. Man's ear is a very complex thing. Its three chambers; the curious characteristics of the innermost of these, with its three "semi-circular canals", its coiled extension, like a snail-shell, called the cochlea, its elaborate nervous mechanism; the membrane between the middle and outer chambers, which vibrates with every pulsation of the air; we can trace all these separate parts as they are added one to one to the auditory apparatus of the evolving race. If we examine the edge of the "umbrella" of the free-swimming Medusa, we shall find some little capsules containing one or more tiny crystals, the homologues of the inner ear; the lower forms of Vermes have similar ears, and in some there are delicate hairs within the capsule which quiver constantly; the higher worms have these capsules paired and they lie close to a mass of nervous matter. Lobsters and their relations have similar ears, the capsule being sometimes closed and sometimes open. In many insects a delicate membrane is added to the auditory apparatus, and stretches between the vesicle and the outer air, homologue of our membrane. The lower fishes have added one semi-circular canal, the next higher two, and the next higher three: a little expansion is also seen at one part of the vesicle. In the frogs and toads this extension is increased, and in the reptiles and birds it is still larger, and is curled a little at the further end. In the lowest mammals it is still only bent, but in the higher it rolls round on itself and forms the cochlea. The reptiles and birds have the space developed between the vesicle and the membrane, and so acquire a middle ear; the crocodile and the owl show a trace of the external ear, but it is not highly developed till we reach the mammals, and even the lowest mammals, and the aquatic ones, have little of it developed. Thus step by step is the ear built up, until we see it complete as a slow growth, not as an intelligent design.

And if it be asked, how are these changes caused, the answer comes readily : "By variation and by the survival of the fittest". Since organisms and their environments re-act on each other, slight variations are constantly occurring; living organisms are ever in very unstable equilibrium, chemical association and disassociation are continually going on within them. Some of these changes are advantageous to the organism in the struggle for existence; some are indifferent; some are disadvantageous. Those that are advantageous tend to persist, since the organism possessing them is more likely to survive than its less fortunate competitors, and — since variations are transmissible from parents to progeny—to hand on its favorable variation to its young. On the other hand the disadvantageous variations tend to disappear, since the organism which is by them placed at a disadvantage is likely to perish in the fight for food. Here are the mighty forces that cause evolution; here the "not ourselves which makes for righteousness", i.e., for ever-increasing suitability of the organism to its environment.

It is, of course, impossible in so brief a statement as this to do justice to the fulness of the explanation of all cases of apparent design which can be made in this fashion. The thoughtful student must work out the line of argument for himself. Nor must he forget to notice the argument from the absence of design, the want of adaptation, the myriad failures, the ineptitudes and incompetences of nature. How, from the point of view of design, can he explain the numerous rudimentary organs in the higher animals? What is the meaning of man's hidden rudimentary tail? of his appendix cœci vermiformis? of the branchial clefts and the lanugo of the human being during periods of ante-natal life? of the erratic course of the recurrent laryngeal? of the communication between the larynx and the alimentary canal? I might extend the list over a page. The fact that uninstructed people do not appreciate these difficulties offers no explanation to the instructed who feel their force; and the abuse so freely lavished on the Atheist does not carry conviction to the intellect.

I do not believe in God. My mind finds no grounds on which to build up a reasonable faith. My heart revolts against the spectre of an Almighty Indifference to the pain of sentient beings. My conscience rebels against the injustice, the cruelty, the inequality, which surround me on every side. But I believe in Man. In man's redeeming power ; in man's remoulding energy ; in man's approaching triumph, through knowledge, love, and work.

Milton Keynes UK
Ingram Content Group UK Ltd.
UKHW030042091224
452079UK00007B/29

9 781535 816014